FLASHCARD   BOOKS

ANIMALS

ENGLISH

to

GERMAN

FLASHCARD   BOOK

BLACK & WHITE EDITION

HOW TO USE:

- READ THE ENGLISH WORD ON THE FIRST PAGE.

- IF YOU KNOW THE TRANSLATION SAY IT OUT LOUD.

- TURN THE PAGE AND SEE IF YOU GOT IT RIGHT.

- IF YOU GUESSED CORRECTLY, WELL DONE!
IF NOT, TRY READING THE WORD USING THE PHONETIC PRONUNCIATION GUIDE.

- NOW TRY THE NEXT PAGE.
THE MORE YOU PRACTICE THE BETTER YOU WILL GET!

BOOKS IN THIS SERIES:
ANIMALS
NUMBERS SHAPES AND COLORS
HOUSEHOLD ITEMS
CLOTHES

ALSO AVAILABLE IN OTHER LANGUAGES INCLUDING:

FRENCH, GERMAN, SPANISH, ITALIAN,

RUSSIAN, CHINESE, JAPANESE AND MORE.

WWW.FLASHCARDEBOOKS.COM

Bat

Die Fledermaus

Fle-der-mouse

Bear

Der Bär

Bear

Bee

Die Biene

Bee-ne

Parakeet

Der Sittich

Sit-ich

Bull

Der Bulle

Bull-eh

Butterfly

Der Schmetterling

Shmett-er-ling

Cheetah

Der Gepard

Geh-part

Chicken

Das Huhn

Hoon

Cow

Die Kuh

Kooh

Crab

Die Krabbe

Krab-beh

Crocodile

Das Krokodil

Croco-deal

Dolphin

Der Delfin

Del-phin

Duck

Die Ente

en-tae

Elephant

Der Elefant

Ele-fun-t

Fish

Der Fisch

Fish

Flamingo

Der Flamingo

Flah-mingo

Fox

Der Fuchs

Fux

Frog

Der Frosch

Frosh

Giraffe

Die Giraffe

Geer-uf-eh

Goat

Die Ziege

Zee-geh

Goose

Die Gans

Guns

Gorilla

Der Gorilla

Gorilla

Hamster

Der Hamster

Hum-ster

Hippo

Das Nilpferd

Nil-fair-d

Horse

Das Pferd

Fair-d

Iguana

Der Leguan

Lay-guan

Jellyfish

Die Qualle

Quall-eh

Kangaroo

Das Känguru

Kang-goo-rooh

Koala

Der Koala

Koala

Ladybird

Der Marienkäfer

Marine-k-fur

Lion

Der Löwe

Low-we

Manatee

Die Seekuh

Seh-kooh

Monkey

Der Affe

Uf-feh

Mouse

Die Maus

Mouse

Ostrich

Der Strauß

Str-ouse

Owl

Die Eule

Eul-eh

Panda

Der Panda

Pun-dah

Parrot

Der Papagei

Pap-uh-guy

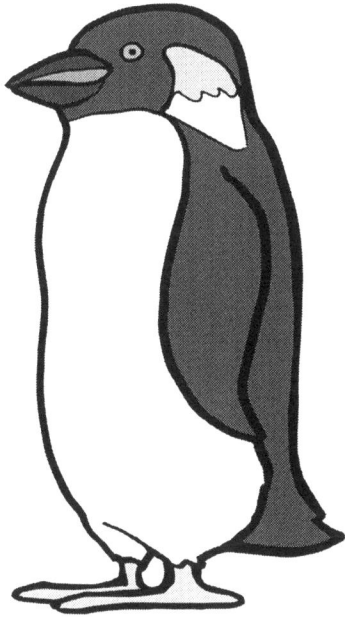

Penguin

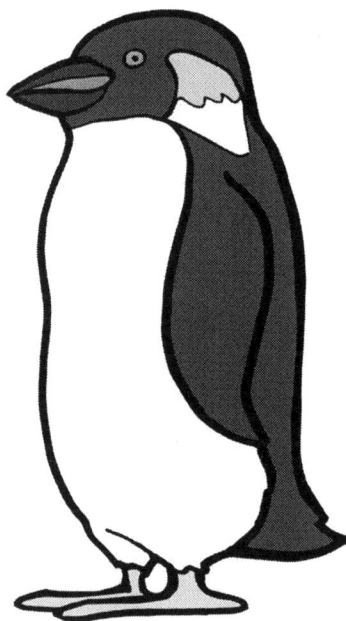

Der Pinguin

Ping-uin

Pigeon

Die Taube

Tau-beh

Pig

Das Schwein

Sh-wine

Rabbit

Der Hase

Ha-seh

Rat

Die Ratte

Rah-teh

Rhino

Das Nashorn

Nas-horn

Rooster

Der Hahn

Huh-n

Scorpion

Der Skorpion

Scorp-ion

Seagull

Die Möwe

Moe-weh

Seal

Die Robbe

Rob-beh

Shark

Der Hai

Hi

Sheep

Das Schaf

Sh-arf

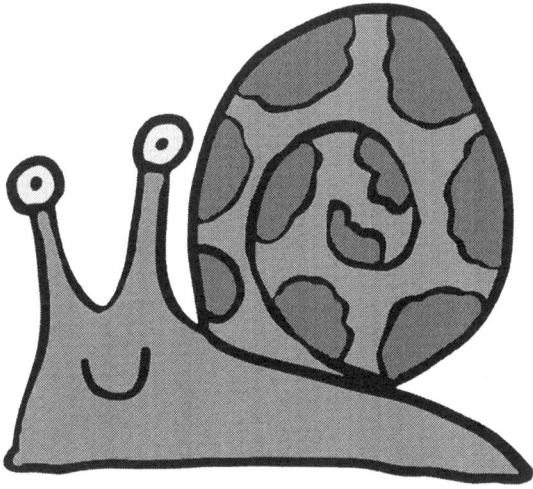

Snail

Die Schnecke

Shnek-eh

Snake

Die Schlange

Shlung-eh

Squirrel

Das Eichhörnchen

Ai-ch-hurn-chen

Stag

Der Hirsch

He-rsh

Stork

Der Storch

Shtor-ch

Tiger

Der Tiger

Tee-ger

Toad

Die Kröte

Kroe-teh

Tortoise

Die Schildkröte

Shill-d-kro-teh

Turkey

Der Truthahn

True-t-hun

Turtle

Die Schildkröte

Shill-d-kro-teh

Wolf

Der Wolf

W-olf

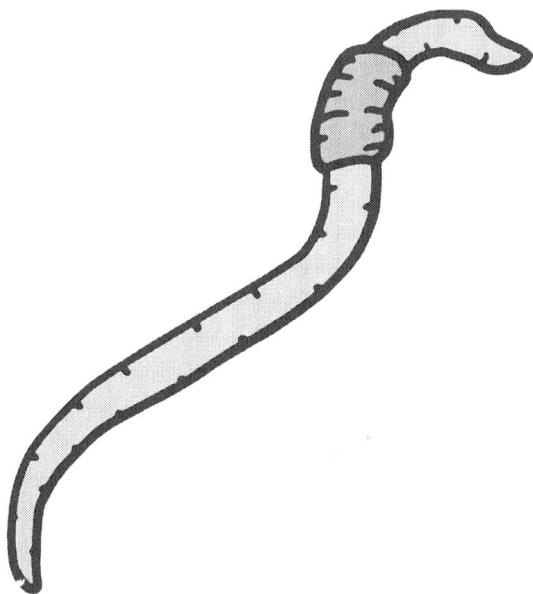

Worm

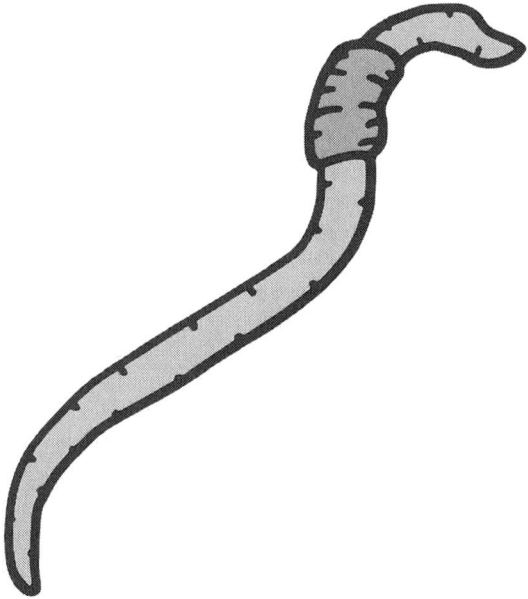

Der Wurm

Wurm